Please Treasure Yourself

Persimmon *(Diospyros virginiana) Plant Illustrations.*
New York Botanical Garden, 1854

PLEASE TREASURE YOURSELF

ZEN POEMS BY
SUSAN F. GLASSMEYER

SHANTI ARTS PUBLISHING
BRUNSWICK, MAINE

PLEASE TREASURE YOURSELF: ZEN POEMS

Copyright © 2025 Susan F. Glassmeyer

All Rights Reserved

No part of this document may be reproduced or transmitted in any form or by any means without prior written permission of the publisher, except in the case of brief quotations embodied in critical reviews.

Published by Shanti Arts Publishing

Designed by Shanti Arts Designs

Cover image—Nakamura Hōchū / National Museum of Asian Art, Smithsonian Institution, Freer Collection, Purchase—Harold P. Stern Memorial Fund, F1996.28

Shanti Arts LLC
193 Hillside Road
Brunswick, Maine 04011
shantiarts.com

Printed in the United States of America

ISBN: 978-1-962082-60-0 (softcover)

LCCN: 2025934587

*For David,
My life partner
and dharma buddy*

Contents

Acknowledgments / 11
Preface / 13

Day 1   Persimmon Lesson
Day 2   Heirloom Lilac
Day 3   Listen
Day 4   Despite Differences
Day 5   Waking Up
Day 6   Body of Patience
Day 7   Two Kinds of Reality
Day 8   Inhale Exhale
Day 9   The Thinking Body
Day 10   Old Woman Suffers

Day 11   Whether the Weather
Day 12   You Say
Day 13   Right Speech
Day 14   Letting Go
Day 15   The Suchness of Things
Day 16   Forgetting It Was Winter
Day 17   It's Not Personal
Day 18   Up North Vacation
Day 19   Neighbor at the Door
Day 20   Practice Anywhere

Day 21   Nothing More Important
Day 22   Scratching the Surface
Day 23   Loneliness
Day 24   Good Question
Day 25   Identity Crisis
Day 26   Walking Alone after Sunset
Day 27   Between Dozing and Thinking
Day 28   Be Surprised
Day 29   I Think, Therefore I Think
Day 30   Nothing to Discuss

Day 31	Choiceless Choice
Day 32	No Ambition
Day 33	The Sky Laughs
Day 34	Sanity
Day 35	Zazen Practice
Day 36	The Cat
Day 37	For Your Consideration
Day 38	Zazen Posture
Day 39	Flesh and Bones
Day 40	Please Treasure Yourself

Day 41	Bubble
Day 42	Wishful Thinking
Day 43	Wake Up to Reality
Day 44	Bored with Meditation?
Day 45	Zazen Is Not a Theory
Day 46	Forget about Time
Day 47	Letting Go
Day 48	Q & A
Day 49	Midwest Zazen
Day 50	Rearranging the Furniture

Day 51	Practice
Day 52	No Separation
Day 53	Responsibility
Day 54	Attitude of Evenness
Day 55	And So It Goes
Day 56	Resting in Nondualism
Day 57	Whether We Know It or Not
Day 58	To Enter Pure Land
Day 59	Poverty of Wealth
Day 60	Peaceable Place

Day 61	IN TRUTH
Day 62	RED! PINK! YELLOW!
Day 63	MIDDLE WAY DHARMA
Day 64	GET USED TO IT
Day 65	PAIN OF PREFERENCE
Day 66	FACT OF LIFE
Day 67	NEAR ACCIDENT
Day 68	TAKING REFUGE
Day 69	TAKING DIRECTION
Day 70	VOW

Day 71	FOR THE WELL-BEING OF ALL
Day 72	BOWING DOWN
Day 73	BEHAVING LIKE AN ADULT
Day 74	WHEEL OF FORTUNE
Day 75	THE NOW THAT IS NOW
Day 76	EITHER WAY
Day 77	NURTURING MIND
Day 78	GOOD PARENTING
Day 79	NO OBSTRUCTION
Day 80	INSTRUCTIONS TO THE DRIVER

Day 81	UNEXPECTED TEACHER
Day 82	ORIENTATION
Day 83	DEAD OR ALIVE
Day 84	MORE GOOD PARENTING
Day 85	MONK SPEAKS
Day 86	DŌGEN ZENJI SAYS
Day 87	MONK SPEAKS AGAIN
Day 88	HIBACHI MONASTERY
Day 89	NO EXCEPTIONS
Day 90	WHOLEHEARTEDLY

NOTES / 65
ABOUT THE AUTHOR / 67

Acknowledgments

I am most grateful to the New York Zen Center for Contemplative Care, founded in 2007 by Sensei Koshin Paley Ellison and Sensei Chodo Robert Campbell, and to their devoted staff who make the mission of the Center possible. It was through my participation in the Center's Commit to Sit program that this book joyfully emerged. To learn more about NYZC, visit www.zencare.org.

A deep bow of thanks to the sixteen visiting teachers from across the world who generously paid tribute to the wisdom of Kōshō Uchiyama Roshi during the Commit to Sit period from June through August, 2023. Heartfelt thanks to the many members of the sangha who gathered to meditate in person at the NYZC zendo, and others (like myself) who participated via the online "zoomdo" for this Commit to Sit period.

Gratitude for my family, friends, and clients who supported me throughout this writing project. Some were early readers, others offered artistic feedback about the bones of this book, notably Professor Loyola Walter, M.F.A. I truly treasure my poet friends David Denny, Jeffrey Hillard, Valerie Chronis Bickett, and Claudia Skutar who have nudged me to do good with my words.

Polishing this manuscript rested in the capable hands of my smart and meticulous editor, Ann Stapleton of Hocking Hills, Ohio. Her attention to detail was impeccable. Her suggestions made my writing better and were always delivered with utter respect and Midwestern kindness.

A deep bow to my independent publisher, Christine Cote of Shanti Arts (Brunswick, Maine) whose valuable work is grounded in nature, art, and spirit. She brought life to my manuscript by recognizing the heart of it, allowing its beauty to shine in the form of this book.

Finally, a long overdue thanks goes to Marge Piercy, poet and author extraordinaire. In the summer of 2012, I was a juried member of a small group of writers who had the good fortune to study poetry under the direction of Marge Piercy on Cape Cod. Her passionate mentoring and personal attention to my poetry imbued me with a sense of confidence that helped me develop my "voice" and resulted in subsequent book publications. I am grateful for this opportunity to thank Marge Piercy publicly for all she has generously given me and so many others.

Preface

These small poems (cinquains) were inspired by daily readings from the book *Opening the Hand of Thought* by Japanese Sōtō Zen priest Kōshō Uchiyama.

The selected readings accompanied a ninety-day sitting meditation period (ango) offered by the New York Zen Center for Contemplative Care from June through August, 2023.

Uchiyama's teachings prompted these distillations and encouraged me to embody his wisdom in day-to-day interactions with others. The opportunity to meditate for three months with an extended community of engaged meditators was a privilege I never took for granted—an opportunity made possible by the efforts of the dedicated founders and staff members of the Center.

In gratitude for their invaluable work, a portion of the proceeds from the sale of *Please Treasure Yourself* will be donated to the NYZC organization so that others may benefit from their compassionate programs.

To learn more about NYZC, visit www.zencare.org.

This old village—
not a single house
without persimmon trees
—Basho

The Persimmon Tree

The Japanese persimmon tree has a long and storied history dating back to the seventh century. It takes many years to grow a sweet persimmon. Depending on the variety of the tree, flowers can take up to five years to emerge, and even longer for trees to bear edible fruit, often up to ten years. The fruit of a persimmon tree that is forty or fifty years old can sometimes still be astringent.

The persimmon is a strange fruit. If you eat it before it is fully ripe, it tastes just awful. Its astringency makes your mouth pucker up. Actually, you can't eat it unripe; if you tried, you would just have to spit it out and throw the whole thing away. Buddhist practice is like this too: if you don't let it really ripen, it cannot nourish your life. That is why I hope that people will begin to practice and then continue until their practice is really ripe.

—Kōshō Uchiyama, *Opening the Hand of Thought*

Day 1

Persimmon Lesson

The orchard

patiently waits.

What's impossible takes sweet

time to ripen and nourish

the fruit.

Day 2

Heirloom Lilac

Planted

before you were born.

Fewer flowers now, but

their reliable scent lingers

in the air.

Day 3

LISTEN

Beeping

city dump truck.

Fading rin gong chime.

Each sound calls me back again

to practice.

Day 4

DESPITE DIFFERENCES

If you

fall to the ground,

may I help you get back up

no matter who you voted for

last time.

Day 5

Waking Up

Pouring

this cup of tea

intentionally,

the pot, the cup, this pourer

cease to be.

Day 6

Body of Patience

Having

washed my face

ten thousand times and more,

today I am feeling it for

the first time.

Day 7

Two Kinds of Reality

Drinking tea

in Cincinnati

could happen, or not.

But dying is a certainty,

like it or not.

Day 8

Inhale Exhale

Since you

have a body,

why hold your breath? If a bird

did that, it would fall

from the sky.

Day 9

The Thinking Body

We cannot

think a thought

without a body. So,

to slow the mind, slow down

the body.

Day 10

Old Woman Suffers

Her son

dropped dead at dawn.

Staring out the window, she

disbelieves the news that he

is gone.

Day 11

Whether the Weather

Whether

it rains on you

or the sun burns brightly,

the sky has no interest in radar

reports.

Day 12

You Say

I hurt you

many years ago.

I believe you, but how

will today's apology ever be

enough?

Day 13

Right Speech

Is there

a way to say

NO wholeheartedly

as when you wholeheartedly

say YES?

Day 14

Letting Go

Tied to

the chair of form,

I tug the ropes that bind me.

Then suddenly—no chair,

no rope, no me!

Day 15

The Suchness of Things

Just be.

Things as they are

are ungraspable anyway.

Right now is all-important, so

just be.

Day 16

Forgetting It Was Winter

Anger

was the black ice

I fast fell down on.

Broken bones, broken vows—

hands so cold.

Day 17

It's Not Personal

Big Self

permeates all

including the small self.

No separation to worry

about.

Day 18

Up North Vacation

Eager

to leave the city,

you watch your well-made plans

lose their importance. Let go

your big ideas.

Day 19

Neighbor at the Door

Come in.

Sit down. Let's have

a look at ourselves.

I've ignored you long enough,

my Friend.

Day 20

Practice Anywhere

No such

place as Japan.

No such place as Ohio.

No such place as America.

Only here.

Day 21

Nothing More Important

All things

being what they are,

plants root deeply,

benefiting generations

going forward.

Day 22

Scratching the Surface

As soon

as I open

my mouth to talk about

enlightenment—it smiles,

goes silent.

Day 23

LONELINESS

If I
set a fine table
for friends, but ask them
to cook the food, we all
stay hungry.

Day 24

GOOD QUESTION

Who do
you think you are?!
Little did he know
his anger offered a lifetime
of inquiry.

Day 25

IDENTITY CRISIS

O wardrobe

of presentations,

how much time is squandered

searching for just the right

outfit.

Day 26

WALKING ALONE AFTER SUNSET

I thought

I was awake,

but a deer bursting by

jolted me out of this self-made

stupor.

Day 27

Between Dozing and Thinking

If I

were truly here

would this poem exist

on the page, or anywhere

at all?

Day 28

Be Surprised

The rock

at water's edge

I attempt to sit down on

is a napping snapping

turtle!

Day 29

I Think, Therefore I Think

Just when

I think I've thought

it all out, along comes

a Japanese monk who says:

Not so fast.

Day 30

Nothing to Discuss

Before

definitions,

what can possibly be

expressed? Your ineffable

true nature.

Day 31

Choiceless Choice

Forget

about your plans.

They'll happen whether or not

you believe you chose them.

Ha!

Day 32

No Ambition

After

so many poems

sought success and found it,

the writer now closes her door

to write.

Day 33

The Sky Laughs

The sun

still shines behind

sudden clouds at sunset.

Cursing reality changes

nothing.

Day 34

Sanity

Living

blindly, I see

I make reality

what I want it to be, but

it's not that.

Day 35

Zazen Practice

Sitting

straight or slouching,

awake or nodding off,

either way, just pay attention

and sit.

Day 36

The Cat

Walks over me

while I meditate.

I'm no more important than

a basket of unfolded

laundry.

Day 37

For Your Consideration

It takes

a book of words

to repeatedly state:

You do not need a book of words.

Do you?

Day 38

Zazen Posture

Blood drains

from the busy head.

Mind begins to quiet.

Thoughts float by on an endless

river.

Day 39

Flesh and Bones

Dear friend,

please stay awake.

Don't doze off in traffic.

Beware the driver who runs

the red light.

Day 40

Please Treasure Yourself

Listen,

do not give up.

Consider that Life is

in service to your brokenness,

always.

Day 41

Bubble

Stop aiming

to rise up

with some purpose in mind.

In an instant, it will simply

vanish.

Day 42

Wishful Thinking

Seeking

freedom from pain

to attain bliss, misses

the point. It only creates

more pain.

Day 43

WAKE UP TO REALITY

Remember,

the scenery

of life is not the play

on the stage of life. It is

just life.

Day 44

BORED WITH MEDITATION?

Death camp

survivor reminds us:

Please don't curse your boredom.

Instead, consider it

a luxury.

Day 45

Zazen Is Not a Theory

Silence

is a practice

inside of a practice.

Not an idea, just something

you do!

Day 46

Forget about Time

Days pass

all by themselves

whether we compare times,

or not. Nothing to dwell on

but this.

Day 47

Letting Go

Thinking

about suffering,

I suffer. Letting go

of thinking about it . . .

less suffering.

Day 48

Q & A

How does

the struggling self

stop struggling?

It's easy if you don't give it

much thought.

Day 49

Midwest Zazen

Outdoor heat

breathes down our necks.

Indoor A/C chills to the bone.

Sweating or shivering,

we just sit.

Day 50

Rearranging the Furniture

The old

view and new view

appear to be different.

And yet, they are also still

the same view.

Day 51

Practice

Ten years

is a long time

to pay attention.

How about ten minutes, ten

seconds.

Day 52

No Separation

When we

hurt each other,

we hurt ourselves. But

the all-inclusive Self does

no harm.

Day 53

Responsibility

One vine

feeds a line of squash.

Nourish the vine, the fruit

flourishes. Neglect it, the fruit

gets squashed.

Day 54

Attitude of Evenness

The bird,

the cat, the cushion.

Through all circumstances

we live out the reality of one

all-pervading life.

Day 55

And So It Goes

Today

began in hell.

Midday was heavenly.

Tonight, it's feeling quite toasty

again.

Day 56

Resting in Nondualism

No need

to create some

new self. And no need

to eliminate the self. Just

let life be.

Day 57

Whether We Know It or Not

We are

all living out

indivisible life—

that which pervades everything,

always.

Day 58

To Enter Pure Land

Chanting

zazen by mouth,

or sitting on the floor

with the whole body—both ways

are the One way.

Day 59

Poverty of Wealth

Wanting

what I want,

then after getting it

wanting something more than before,

I remain poor.

Day 60

Peaceable Place

Can peace

be possible

without pursuing it?

Can what comes to the quiet mind

be peace?

Day 61

In Truth

If done

wholeheartedly,

scrubbing out the toilet,

pumping gas, making love . . .

it's all zazen.

Day 62

Red! Pink! Yellow!

Today's

hibiscus plant

blossoms in three colors!

No explanation but for life's

vigor.

Day 63

Middle Way Dharma

Staying

wide awake,

I can better see

how thinking in extremes causes

trouble.

Day 64

Get Used to It

It comes

and then it goes.

The ceaseless river flows.

We are in it. We are with it.

We are it.

Day 65

Pain of Preference

A trace

of this or that,

the pursuit of outcome.

Cherishing opinions keeps me

caged.

Day 66

Fact of Life

As the world

constantly shifts,

the head wants to label

everything. Even in my sleep

I name things.

Day 67

Near Accident

It was

not my day to die.

I took it all in stride.

So after I drove home, I just

sat still.

Day 68

Taking Refuge

Enter

your inner room.

Take a seat. Be quiet.

Everything else passes away

but this.

Day 69

Taking Direction

Acting

in accordance

with all that surrounds me,

absolute peace follows

such a vow.

Day 70

Vow

Caring

for my own life,

I take care of the world.

In doing so, the light of Buddha

burns bright.

Day 71

For the Well-Being of All

You say

bodhisattva.

I say regular guy.

Either way, let's just be kind

to each other.

Day 72

Bowing Down

Sometimes

surrendering

without an explanation,

or apology, is best for

all concerned.

Day 73

Behaving Like an Adult

When I

get all mixed up

I listen to my inner

bodhisattva, then take her good

advice.

Day 74

Wheel of Fortune

Take heed!

We cry for money

from the game show of life.

Then we cry again after we

get it.

Day 75

The Now That Is Now

Forget

the past. Forget

the future. Neither one

exists because everything comes

and goes.

Day 76

Either Way

Whether

heaven be my life,

or whether it be hell,

is there a way to simply

live it?

Day 77

Nurturing Mind

The past

and the future

exist in the present.

No heaven or hell. Just the scenery

of life.

Day 78

Good Parenting

Be kind.

Exclude nothing!

Everyone and everything

blossoms under your watchful eye.

No exceptions!

Day 79

No Obstruction

Practice

without a thought.

Just as the sky moves out

of cloud's way, move out of

your own way.

Day 80

Instructions to the Driver

Braking

the car on ice

creates dangerous sliding.

Steering into the slide offers

relief.

Day 81

Unexpected Teacher

Dear rose,

be my sensei.

Your stem, your bud, all

your many petals, even your

sharp thorns.

Day 82

Orientation

Posture

is not only

about physical form.

Posture of the mind itself

matters.

Day 83

Dead or Alive

Your face

in the mirror

as well as your face before

your parents were born ... how can you

live both?

Day 84

More Good Parenting

Think big.

Forgive yourself.

Reduce acquired karma.

Open the Hand, the Heart, the Mind.

Bring Joy!

Day 85

Monk Speaks

If you

vow to live out

your life wherever you are,

sooner or later spring will come,

and blossom.

Day 86

Dōgen Zenji Says

Only

a fool regards

oneself as another.

A wise one regards others as

oneself.

Day 87

Monk Speaks Again

Just sit.

Sit silently

for ten years. Then another

ten years. Then just sit for the rest of

your life.

Day 88

Hibachi Monastery

Alone,

the fire goes out.

But where two or more coals

are gathered together, flames

grow bright.

Day 89

No Exceptions

Whether

we think so or not,

everything is one with

everything, including our Life,

and Death.

Day 90

Wholeheartedly

In Life,

dance in the sun

so that in Death we may lie

cheerfully in the shadows

of the grass.

Notes

Ango—

Ango is a Japanese term for a three-month period of committed meditation practice and engaged study for students of Zen Buddhism. The word ango literally translates as "dwelling in peace." In current times, Zen centers may allow members of an active ango to participate flexibly so they can continue to work and fulfill other obligations throughout the day.

Cinquain—

The cinquain is a poem composed of five lines. The origin of the form dates back to medieval French poetry. The American Cinquain, developed by early twentieth century poet Adelaide Crapsey, consists of eleven stresses distributed among the five lines in a 1, 2, 3, 4, and 1 pattern, respectively. Adelaide Crapsey's cinquains share a similarity with the Japanese tanka, another five-line poetic form.

Dharma—

The word dharma has many meanings, but here it refers to the teachings of the historical Buddha—the universal truth common to all individuals.

Dōgen Zenji—

A Japanese Buddhist priest, writer, poet, philosopher, and founder of the Sōtō school of Zen in Japan (1200–1253).

Sangha—

A Sanskrit word meaning a community of people practicing right conduct and behavior together to bring about and to maintain awareness, understanding, acceptance, harmony, and compassion.

Sensei—

A Japanese title for a venerable teacher, master, or professional.

Zazen—

The practice of single-minded, unremitting seated meditation, also referred to as "just sitting" (shikantaza).

Zendo—

A room or hall where sitting meditation (zazen) is practiced.

About the Author

SUSAN F. GLASSMEYER is Codirector of the Holistic Health Center of Cincinnati where she works as a somatic therapist and Feldenkrais® Practitioner, helping people heal from trauma in order to experience the poetry of presence in their bodies. Susan was named Ohio Poet of the Year for her 2018 collection *Invisible Fish* (Dos Madres Press). She is also the author of *Four Blue Eggs: American Cinquains* (Little Pocket Poetry Press), *Body Matters* (Pudding House Press), and *Cook's Luck* (Finishing Line Press). Her poems have appeared in *Rattle*, *JAMA*, *Naugatuck River Review*, *Dunes Review*, *Pulse*, *Pine Mountain Sand & Gravel*, *Grateful Living* (grateful.org), and other print and online journals. She is a longtime member of the Greater Cincinnati Writers League and Ohio Poetry Association, and is the creator of April Gifts, a ten-year poetry project honoring National Poetry Month. Susan traces the roots of her interest in both meditation and poetry to early childhood when her railroad worker grandfather taught her to pay close attention to the language of train whistles.

To learn more, visit www.susanglassmeyer.com.

Shanti Arts

Nature • Art • Spirit

Please visit us online
to browse our entire book catalog,
including poetry collections and fiction,
books on travel, nature, healing, art,
photography, and more.

Also take a look at our highly regarded art
and literary journal, *Still Point Arts Quarterly*,
which may be downloaded for free.

www.shantiarts.com

www.ingramcontent.com/pod-product-compliance
Lightning Source LLC
LaVergne TN
LVHW041346080426
835512LV00006B/641